W9-BKU-820
0 1021 0166872 5

Masterpieces: Artists and Their Works

Monet

by Shelley Swanson Sateren

Consultant:
Joan Lingen, Ph.D.
Professor of Art History
Clarke College
Dubuque, Iowa

Bridgestone Books
an imprint of Capstone Press
Mankato, Minnesota

Bridgestone Books are published by Capstone Press
151 Good Counsel Drive, P.O. Box 669, Mankato, Minnesota 56002
http://www.capstone-press.com

Printed in the United States of America.

Library of Congress Cataloging-in-Publication Data

Sateren, Shelley Swanson.

Monet/by Shelley Swanson Sateren.

p. cm.—(Masterpieces: artists and their works)

Includes bibliographical references and index.

Summary: Discusses the personal life and artistic accomplishments of Impressionist Claude Monet.

ISBN 0-7368-1123-0

1. Monet, Claude, 1840–1926—Juvenile literature. 2. Painters—France—Biography—Juvenile literature. [1. Monet, Claude, 1840-1926. 2. Artists. 3. Painting, French.] I. Title. II. Series.

ND553.M7 S3 2002

759.4—dc21 2001003738

Editorial Credits

Blake Hoena, editor; Karen Risch, product planning editor; Heather Kindseth, cover and interior layout designer; Katy Kudela, photo researcher

Photo Credits

Archivo Iconografico, S.A./CORBIS, cover (left)

Fogg Art Museum, Harvard University Museums, USA/Bequest from the collection of Maurice Wertheim, Class 1906/Bridgeman Art Library, 12; Gift of Mr. and Mrs. Joseph Pulitzer/Bridgeman Library, 16

Musee des Beaux-Arts, Nantes, France/Giraudon-Bridgeman Art Library, 20 (top)

Musee Marmottan, Paris, France/Giraudon-Bridgeman Art Library, 10

Musee d'Orsay, Paris, France/Roger-Viollet, Paris/Bridgeman Art Library, 4; Giraudon-Bridgeman Art Library, 8, 14 (bottom)

National Gallery, London, UK/Bridgeman Art Library, 18

National Gallery of Scotland, Edinburgh, Scotland/Bridgeman Art Library, 14 (top)

Private Collection/Bridgeman Art Library, 6; Roger-Viollet, Paris/Bridgeman Art Library, 20 (bottom)

Roger-Viollet/Getty Images, cover (right)

1 2 3 4 5 6 07 06 05 04 03 02

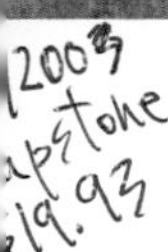

Table of Contents

Claude Monet is one of the most famous Impressionists. He painted this painting, *Self Portrait,* of himself in 1917.

Claude Monet

Claude Monet (1840–1926) was a French artist. He and his artist friends invented a style of art called Impressionism.

Impressionists did not paint pictures that looked real. Instead, they tried to paint scenes the way they looked at a quick glance. They did this in part by using broken brush strokes.

Claude also became one of the first artists to paint mainly outdoors. For centuries, artists made rough sketches of outdoor scenes. They then painted indoors while looking at their drawings.

In his outdoor paintings, Claude showed how light and color changed. He often painted objects in series. These paintings showed the same scene at a different time of day or season. Claude is best known for his haystack series and water lily series.

Throughout his life, Claude painted many outdoor scenes. He painted *Route de Chailly, Fontainebleu* in 1864.

Young Claude

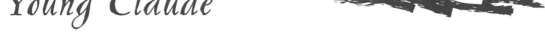

Oscar-Claude Monet was born in Paris, France, on November 14, 1840. He was the second child of Claude and Louise Monet.

When Claude was 5 years old, his family moved to Le Havre. This port town lies on the northern coast of France. Claude enjoyed the sea. He often watched fishers at work and made drawings of their ships.

At age 14, Claude began to draw caricatures of well-known people in Le Havre. An art shop owner displayed these funny pictures in his store window. Claude felt proud when people began to buy his drawings.

In 1856, an artist named Eugene Boudin visited Le Havre. He saw Claude's drawings in the shop window and was impressed by them. Boudin invited Claude to paint with him outdoors. Claude spent one day painting with Boudin. He then knew he wanted to be an artist.

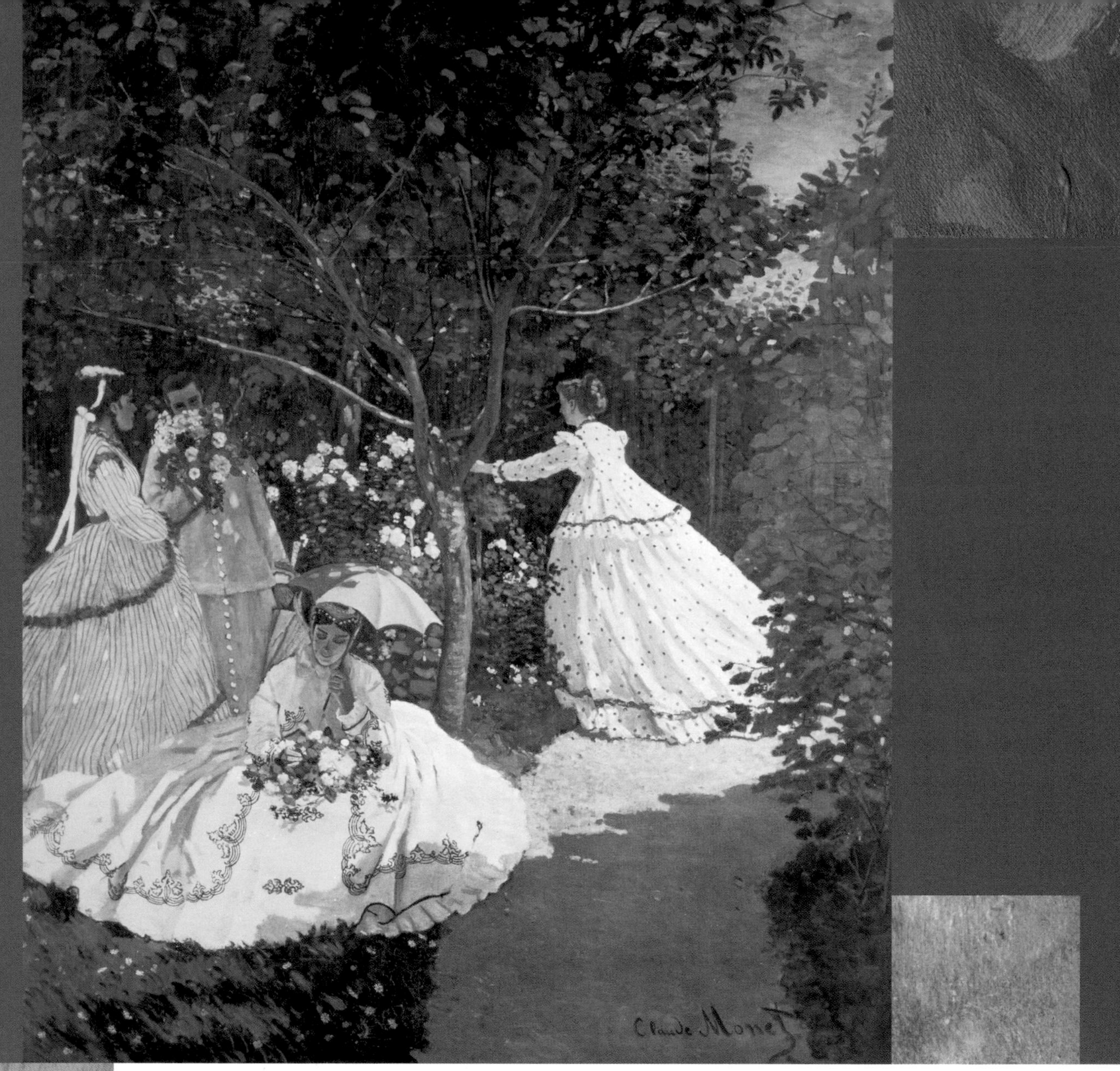

Claude had Camille model for *Women in the Garden*. He used her image for three of the four figures in the painting.

Paris

In 1859, Claude moved back to Paris. His aunt, Marie-Jeanne Lecadre, gave him money to study art there. In Paris, he met, studied, and talked with several young artists.

Claude also met Camille Doncieux in Paris. She modeled for many of his paintings. In 1867, Claude and Camille had a son named Jean. In 1870, they married.

The Salon was a famous art gallery in Paris. Every year, it held a large art exhibit. Artists could submit paintings to the Salon for display.

In 1866, the Salon accepted two of Claude's paintings. One of the paintings was called *Women in the Garden*. The painting stood more than 8 feet (2.4 meters) tall. Claude created this work outdoors. He dug a trench and lowered the painting into it. He then could work on the top of the painting. Art critics praised Claude for his works exhibited at the Salon.

Claude displayed *Impression, Sunrise* at an exhibit in 1874. The word "Impressionist" was used to describe all the artists involved in the exhibit.

Impressionism

It was difficult for Claude and his friends to get modern art displayed at the Salon. Many people did not understand their work. Claude and his friends did not paint scenes that looked real. Art critics often thought their paintings were messy and childlike.

In 1874, Claude and some other artists decided to have their own art exhibit. They wanted to show modern styles of art to the public. Artists such as Paul Cézanne, Edgar Degas, and Auguste Renoir took part in this exhibit. These artists became known as Impressionists.

Impressionists wanted to capture a quick glance of the landscapes they painted. They painted in broken brush strokes of one solid color. They painted different colors next to each other without mixing them. In this way, the viewer's eye could mix the colors. Impressionists' paintings look splotchy up close. But from a distance, the pictures seem clearer.

In 1877, Claude painted *The Gare Saint-Lazare: Arrival of a Train.* Train station workers helped him by stopping trains and loading train engines with coal to create smoke.

Struggles

In the 1870s, Claude sold few paintings. He often had to borrow money from friends for food and art supplies.

In 1876, an art collector named Ernest Hoschede hired Claude to do some paintings. Claude became friends with the Hoschede family. But by 1877, Ernest had lost most of his money. He was unable to help Claude any more. Ernest also left his wife, Alice, at this time.

Also in 1877, Claude began to paint several works at the Saint-Lazare train station. The invention of oil paints in tubes allowed him to paint outside his studio. Before this invention, it was difficult to paint outdoors. Artists had to mix their own paints. They made paint by mixing oil with pigments. Pigments are colored substances. For example, an artist might have used blueberry juice to make blue paint.

Claude created many paintings of haystacks. In 1891, he painted *Haystacks: Snow Effect* (top) and *The Haystacks (bottom)*, or *The End of the Summer.*

Haystacks

In 1878, Claude and Camille rented a house with Alice and her six children. That same year, Camille gave birth to her and Claude's second son, Michel.

In 1879, Camille became ill and died. It was a difficult time for Claude. His wife's death saddened him. He also struggled to sell his paintings and had little money. But Alice helped take care of his children so he could continue to paint.

Claude painted mostly outdoors during this time. He created many paintings quickly. He did not worry about how realistic the objects in his paintings looked. Instead, he concentrated on light and color.

Claude painted many of the same scenes at different times of the day. He often worked for an hour or less on one painting. He then worked on another painting of the same scene when the sunlight changed. Claude's haystack paintings were done this way.

Claude often painted the cliffs near Etretat, France. This painting is titled *La Porte d'Amont, Etretat*.

Giverny

In the early 1880s, Claude began to sell more paintings. He eventually earned enough money to rent a house in the village of Giverny near Paris. In 1883, Alice and her children moved there with Claude and his children.

Alice agreed to care for the children in the new home. Claude then was able to travel. Claude traveled in France and other European countries. He painted nature scenes wherever he went.

Claude mostly used bright colors and no black in his paintings. He hardly mixed the paints he used. Dabs of white paint gave movement to water scenes. He also painted in broken brush strokes.

Painting outdoors sometimes was difficult for Claude. He could only work while the sun was shining. He often had to carry his art supplies through snow and down steep cliffs. One day, a large wave threw him against a cliff. He lost his art supplies and nearly drowned.

Claude owned a large water lily pond. He built a Japanese-style bridge over the pond. This painting is titled *The Waterlily Pond.*

Water Lilies

Cla[illegible] lanted flowers and vegetables at the house
in C[illegible] oved gardening and often created
pa[illegible]

[illegible] sold enough paintings
[illegible] en hired workers to

[illegible] rnest, died. In 1892,
[illegible], Claude painted mostly
[illegible] d from sunrise until

[illegible] ude painted his water lily
[illegible] 1916, he began a series of
[illegible] Some of these paintings were
[illegible] ters) wide.
[illegible] large water lily paintings in
[illegible] sell them. They still hung in his
[illegible] n December 5, 1926. Claude was

Claude painted many large water lily paintings. He painted *Waterlilies at Giverny* (top) in 1917.

Monet's Paintings Today

Claude's huge water lily paintings now hang in two rooms at the Orangerie Museum in Paris. Years ago, the king of France used these two oval rooms as a greenhouse. The museum hung the paintings there the year after Claude died.

After Claude's death, his youngest son, Michel, inherited the house at Giverny. Michel also received his father's unsold paintings. When Michel died, he left his father's paintings to the Marmottan Museum in Paris. The house and gardens at Giverny became a museum. Thousands of people visit them every year.

In 1995, the Art Institute of Chicago held an exhibit. The museum gathered 159 of Claude's paintings and drawings from around the world. Thousands of people visited this exhibit.

Today, museums in Paris and Boston own large collections of Claude's paintings. Museums in Chicago and Ottawa, Ontario, also have collections of his art.

Important Dates

1840—Claude is born on November 14.

1856—Eugene Boudin visits Le Havre.

1859—Claude moves to Paris to study art.

1866—Claude has two of his paintings accepted at the Salon.

1867—Claude's first son, Jean, is born.

1870—Claude marries Camille Doncieux.

1874—Claude takes part in the first Impressionist exhibit.

1878—Claude's second son, Michel, is born.

1879—Camille dies.

1883—Claude rents the house at Giverny.

1892—Claude marries Alice Hoschede.

1911—Alice dies.

1914—World War I (1914-1918) begins; Jean dies later in the war.

1926—Claude dies at Giverny on December 5.

Words to Know

caricature (KA-ri-kuh-chur)—an exaggerated, funny drawing of someone

critic (KRIT-ik)—someone who reviews art, books, or movies

exhibit (eg-ZIB-it)—a public display that people visit

Impressionism (im-PREH-shuh-ni-zuhm)—an art style in which artists use broken brush strokes to paint a scene the way it looks at a quick glance

landscape (LAND-skape)—a painting, drawing, or photograph of an outdoor scene

pigment (PIG-muhnt)—a colored substance artists use to make paint

series (SIHR-eez)—a number of works about the same subject

Read More

Connolly, Sean. *Claude Monet.* The Life and Work of. Des Plaines, Ill.: Heinemann Library, 2000.

Kelley, True. *Claude Monet: Sunshine and Waterlilies.* New York: Grosset & Dunlap, 2001.

Malam, John. *Claude Monet.* Tell me about. Minneapolis: Carolrhoda Books, 1998.

Useful Addresses

Museum of Fine Arts, Boston
Avenue of the Arts
465 Huntington Avenue
Boston, MA 02115-5523

National Gallery of Canada
380 Sussex Drive
Box 427, Station A
Ottawa, ON K1N 9N4
Canada

Internet Sites

Monet at Giverny
http://www.mmfa.qc.ca/visite-vr/anglais/index.html
Monet in the 20th Century
http://www.boston.com/mfa/monet/exhibit/exhibit.shtml
WebMuseum, Paris–Monet
http://www.oir.ucf.edu/wm/paint/auth/monet

Index